Chrysanthemums and dahlias

D1147718

Cover:
Chrysanthemum 'Red Lilian Hoek', photograph by Michael Warren

Overleaf:
'Claire de Lune', a collerette dahlia.

Chrysanthemums and dahlias

Wisley handbook

Derek Bircumshaw
Philip Damp

Cassell Ltd

The Royal Horticultural Society

Cassell Ltd.
1 Vincent Square
London, SW1P 2PN
for the Royal Horticultural Society

First published 1986

British Library Cataloguing in Publication Data

Bircumshaw, Derek
  Chrysanthemums and dahlias. — (Wisley
  handbook)
  1. Chrysanthemums   2. Dahlias
  I. Title   II. Damp, Philip   III. Series
  635.9′3355   SB413.C55

ISBN 0-304-31120-0

Line drawings by Sue Wickison
Photographs by Derek Bircumshaw, Philip Damp, Michael
Warren, Holland and Clark, Martyn Rix.

Phototypesetting by Georgia Origination Ltd, Formby
Printed by Het Volk n.v. Ghent, Belgium

Contents

Chrysanthemums

Introduction

A BRIEF HISTORY

The name 'chrysanthemum' comes from two Greek words, *chrysos* meaning gold, and *anthos*, a flower – 'gold flower' as this was the colour of the most popular one in that part of the world. However, there has been much difference of opinion concerning the exact origin of the chrysanthemum, and it is difficult to discover whether they were first cultivated in China or in Japan. The Chinese philosopher Confucius referred to them in some of his writings about 500 B.C. but very soon after that time there are reports of them being grown extensively in Japan. Since then they have been grown in great numbers in Japan where they have been profusely illustrated in books, on fabrics and many religious carvings. The leading growers in Japan are held in great esteem and the popularity of the chrysanthemum has increased through the centuries so much that it is now the official national flower of that country.

There are many species of chrysanthemums grown all over the world and various countries have their own indigenous species but there is no doubt that the popular 'florists' types grown in the British Isles over the last hundred years are descendants of *Chrysanthemum indicum* and *Chrysanthemum sinense*, both natives of the Far East.

Chrysanthemums first came to Europe in 1789 when a French navigator named Louis Blanchard brought some back to Marseilles from a trip to Macao in China. Only one variety, known as 'Old Purple' survived, but stock from it soon reached the Royal Botanic Gardens, Kew. This attracted considerable interest to the species, and when Robert Fortune was commissioned by the Royal Horticultural Society in 1843 to travel to China in search of rare plants, he returned with many more types. Very soon British enthusiasts were raising their own seedlings and were showing them in competition against each other.

The first Chrysanthemum Society was formed in Stoke Newington in 1846. This was the forerunner of the present

National Society and eventually in 1884 changed its name to The National Chrysanthemum Society. This Society has continued to flourish over the years and has several thousand members and affiliated societies throughout the world. It has continued with its objective, namely, to promote the cultivation of chrysanthemums through the publication of specialist books and the organisation of shows and conferences. Membership of this society is recommended to all growers of chrysanthemums whatever type (*see* p. 32).

There is no doubt that the popularity of the chrysanthemum increases year by year and a contributory factor to this upsurge of interest is the versatility of the flower. Coupled with the immense improvement in quality of the cultivars available during the past decade, it is apparent that good flowers of many different types can be produced with reasonable ease by the amateur gardener from August right through to Christmas. Chrysanthemums will adapt themselves to almost any condition, grow in most types of soil, are fairly hardy, and require only a minimum amount of heat during propagation or flowering; in these days of high heating costs this can be a deciding factor. With good common sense gardening all types of these fascinating flowers can be grown; there are no hidden mysteries in their culture and if I were to be asked to put in a nutshell a recipe for successful growing I would say – 'Doing the right thing at the right time.'

Much of the popularity of the chrysanthemum can be attributed to the fact that it blooms when so many summer flowers are in their decline, and also for its marvellous keeping qualities. Chrysanthemums will give a beautiful display of autumn tints in the garden for several weeks, whilst a vase of cut flowers can be kept fresh in the house for almost three weeks with only an occasional change of water.

The arrival of so many excellent cultivars of spray chrysanthemum during the last fifteen years, and the improvement in these types during that time, has meant that they are also popular with flower arrangers.

CLASSIFICATION OF FLOWERS

The different types of florists' chrysanthemums are divided into sections according to flower shapes with each being given a number. They are also categorised depending on whether they are early flowering (for the garden in August or September) or late flowering (for greenhouse in November and December). Those flowering in-between are classified as October flowering. The main types are then sub-divided into three sizes:–

1. Large flowering – these are given the letter (a)
2. Medium flowering – these are given the letter (b)
3. Small flowering – these are given the letter (c)

The chief concern of this book is the kind of chrysanthemum known generally as the florists' type which is grown chiefly for use as a cut flower, or for exhibition. Two smaller categories, the annual type, which is grown from seed, or the hardy herbaceous type, which is often grown in a mixed herbaceous border, are mentioned briefly on pp. 34 and 35.

Spray chrysanthemums have a letter following the number which denotes type of flower in the spray, thus:–

(a) = anemone type
(b) = pompon
(c) = reflex type
(d) = single
(e) = intermediate
(f) = spider quills or spoon type

This may seem complicated but growers of chrysanthemums will need to know these sections in order to read a catalogue and understand the types of flower that are being offered for sale. The types are identified as follows:–

Late flowering chrysanthemums

Section 1. Large exhibition
  (often referred to as Japs)
Section 2. Medium exhibition
Section 3. Incurved
Section 4. Reflexing

Section 5. Intermediate

Section 6. Anemone
Section 7. Singles
Section 8. Pompons
Section 9. Sprays
Section 10. Spiders, Quills and
  Spoons
Section 12. Charms and
  Cascades

Early flowering chrysanthemums

Section 23. Incurved
Section 24. Reflexing
Section 25. Intermediate
Section 26. Anemone

Section 27. Singles
Section 28. Pompons
Section 29. Sprays

An 'incurved' flower type is almost spherical, with the florets curving inwards and upwards. The 'reflexing' types have florets which curve outwards and then downwards towards the stem giving a mushroom type flower. 'Intermediates' are, as it were,

Opposite: Above, 'Pennine Wine', an early flowering spray type.
Below, 'Pennine Ace', an early flowering spoon type.
Above: A general view of the Wisley trials.

half way between incurved and reflexing. Despite being of globular formation as a rule they do not finish over on the top like a ball as the incurves do, but have an open top whereby the inside of the floret is visible. 'Singles' have florets of daisy-like form with a central disc whilst 'anemones' have daisy-like florets but their predominant feature is a cushion-like centre. A 'spray' is really like a complete branch, bearing a number of small blooms where no disbudding has taken place.

The early flowering types are planted out in the garden during May and there they stay, providing flowers through September and early October. Late flowering types (often referred to as greenhouse or indoor chrysanthemums) are grown in pots. They stand outside during the summer months and are carried into a greenhouse during the later part of September to protect them from frost. There they will flower before Christmas.

SELECTION AND TREATMENT OF STOOLS

For the reader who has not grown chrysanthemums before, plants should be ordered from a reputable specialist chrysanthemum nurseryman for delivery in February or March. (For treatment of new plants see pp. 17). However, anyone who has been growing chrysanthemums for some time will already have stock and here the most vigorous selection must take place. Only plants that were in excellent health and gave first class flowers should be retained.

After flowering, the main stem of the plant should be cut down to about 8 inches (20 cm) in height with a pair of secateurs during mid-October. These cut down plants and their roots are called 'stools', and are kept under cover over the winter.

Lift each stool carefully with a small garden fork. A couple of taps on the fork will soon remove all surplus soil and the stool is ready for boxing. Tomato trays are ideal for this job. It is an important task and one not to be taken lightly. Three golden rules should be observed during this process:–

1. Use a good compost
2. Do not bury the stools too deep
3. Do not water in when the job is completed

A John Innes No. 1 potting compost is ideal and this should be spread over the bottom of the tray to a depth of about 2 inches (5 cm). Trim all growth from the stool; this must be done with secateurs and not pulled with thumb and finger otherwise irreparable damage may be done to the base of the stool. Stand the stools side by side on the layer of compost (about 12–15 per tray),

Incurved disbudded flower.

Reflexing disbudded flower.

Chrysanthemum stool; the new
shoots will appear from around
the base.

'Yellow Hammer', a fine example of a Charm chrysanthemum.

then just sprinkle some compost down between the stools. Do not bury them too deep but rather have the stems standing up above the soil. *They should not be watered in.* More stools are lost throughout the winter because they are too wet, than for any other reason. Providing the compost used is just damp, this, together with the moisture already in the stool, will suffice to see it through its rest period. The boxes are then placed in the cold frame and there they will remain for the next two to three months. They should be sprinkled with slug pellets and throughout the ensuing weeks given as much air as possible when weather conditions allow. They remain in the frame until January. They need this period of cold while growth has stopped. An unexpected degree or two of frost will not hurt them as the sap in the chrysanthemum does not freeze until the temperature drops to 28°F (−1° to

'Yvonne Arnaud', an early reflexing chrysanthemum of medium size.

– 2 °C). The stools may be brought into the greenhouse any time after Christmas. They should then be watered and given a little heat. A temperature of 45°F (7°C) will suffice. After being cold and dry in the frame, the combination of heat and moisture starts the stool into growth and very soon new green shoots appear from around the base. This is the vital cutting material the grower is looking for as these shoots are the basis of the plants for the coming season. Ample material should be available three or four weeks after the stools have been given the water and heat.

Propagation

Chrysanthemums can be propagated either by cuttings or by division. Ninety-nine per cent of chrysanthemums are grown from cuttings and this method gives the most vigorous and healthy plant. All that can be said about dividing is that the old stools, after they have made some growth, are divided, just as with any other perennial plant. These are referred to as 'Irishmans cuttings' and all that is necessary is to ensure that each divided growth has some root attached.

TAKING CUTTINGS

Chrysanthemum cuttings will root in almost any medium, although a small propagator will speed up the process. A traditional John Innes rooting compost, or soil-less medium will suffice as will any home-made mixture of almost any combination of loam, peat, grit, coarse sand or Perlite. My personal preference is for a compost containing some proportion of loam. The reason behind this is that the plants are going to be grown in loam in the garden so why not get them used to it from the beginning? Cuttings are usually rooted 35 to a seed tray, and if possible the compost should be warmed up in the greenhouse for a few days prior to insertion. It is most important that the cutting material used on the old roots is in a nice soft vegetative state; old and rather dark-looking shoots should be avoided. Cuttings growing from around the base of the stool are preferable but if these are not present then those growing out of the stem can be used. A cutting should not be too thin and drawn, nor too fat. A cutting trimmed to $1\frac{1}{2}$ inches (3.5 cm) long is ideal with the cut being made just below a leaf joint. The bottom leaf is then taken off and the cutting dipped in a half strength solution of pirimicarb insecticide spray. The lower $\frac{1}{4}$ inch (6 mm) of the stem is then dipped into hormone rooting powder and the cutting is inserted into a small hole made in the compost with the top of a pencil or similar instrument. The cuttings are inserted 35 to a seed tray (7 rows of 5), thoroughly watered in with tepid water, and ideally should be placed over a soil-warming cable in a propagator. It is suggested that cuttings should be taken from mid-February onwards, whilst emphasising that those of the spray cultivars need not be taken until the last two weeks in March.

THE NEXT MOVE

The time a cutting takes to root will vary according to conditions. I have known them to root in ten days and yet the process can take up to a month. A gentle tug on the cutting will show whether it is rooted and the next stage is to take the tray out of the propagator to prevent the cuttings from becoming drawn. Leave the trays of cuttings on a greenhouse shelf in good light for a few days before giving them the next move. After this time chrysanthemums will be quite happy in a temperature of 45–50°F (7–10°C). They need very little heat and will flourish in cool conditions.

It is at this stage that the plants (and I believe we should call them plants as they now have roots) receive somewhat different treatment according to whether they are 'earlies' or 'lates'.

Early flowering cultivars should be moved on into boxes. These must be a little deeper than the standard seed tray; tomato trays or fish boxes are ideal. Twelve to a tomato tray will suffice, but if room can be afforded and only eight put in better results will ensue as the resulting plant and root system will be so much stronger. John Innes No. 2 compost is ideal for this job and the 'earlies' remain in these boxes until planted out into the garden during May. Watering is curtailed at this time and plants should only be given water when they really need a drink. After every watering they should be allowed to dry out before being watered again. A good root system will be encouraged by giving a thorough watering at relatively long intervals.

By the beginning of April plants can be placed out in the cold frame but old matting or sacking should be used to cover the lights should severe frosts be forecast. Chrysanthemums will stand a degree or two of frost but should be protected from severe frosts. Give plenty of ventilation to plants in the frames when conditions allow.

The plants of 'lates' should be potted on into $3\frac{1}{2}$ inch (9 cm) pots – they may be of plastic of clay, but in any case they should be scrubbed clean before use. Allow clay pots to soak overnight before potting so that they are fully charged with water. This will allow a longer interval between potting up and the first watering of the plant; follow the same instructions as for watering the 'earlies' (see above). After 4 to 5 weeks the $3\frac{1}{2}$ inch (9 cm) pots should be filled with roots and the plants moved on into 5 inch (12 cm) pots. The process is just the same, only the compost mixture should contain more nutrient, John Innes No. 3 is advocated. Immediately after this move, the plants will benefit from the cool conditions of a garden frame.

If chrysanthemum plants have been ordered from a specialist

17

nursery they will arrive by post during March and April. They should be short-jointed plants with a good root system and on receipt can be boxed or potted up according to type. Examine the growing tip to see that this has not been damaged in the post and if the roots have dried out at all in transit soak them in water for a few hours before boxing.

The large green leaves of chrysanthemums seem to hold a particular attraction for greenfly and leaf miners; these are the two main pests that attack them and they often become active during April. It is advisable therefore, whilst the plants are in the frames, to spray them regularly as a deterrent. Don't wait until plants are infested – by then the damage has been done. Spray regularly with a pirimicarb-based insecticide (see also p. 28) and ensure the plants are kept clean and healthy.

PLANTING OUT

Depending on the geographical location early flowering chrysanthemums can be planted out at any time between about 7 and 20 May; the danger of severe frosts has usually passed by then. However, before this can be done the piece of ground where they are to be grown has to be prepared. Ideally it will have been rough dug during the winter and humus incorporated. During April, as soon as conditions allow, the lumps are knocked down with a rake and the ground worked into a nice tilth. Don't venture on if the soil sticks to your boots as the soil 'structure' will be destroyed. The top 4 to 5 (10–12 cm) of soil can then be lightly forked over and a base dressing of fertilizer incorporated. A balanced fertilizer, i.e. one with equal proportions of nitrogen, phosphates and potash (N, P_2O_5, K_2O) is most suitable. My own preference is for Eclipse Semi-Organic Fertilizer as chrysanthemums seem to thrive particularly well on this, and I find that 'organics' are much better than man made chemical fertilizers. This can be applied at the rate of 4 oz. to a square yard (115 g per 0.8 m²) about ten days before planting out.

Before planting, a strong 4 to 5 ft (1.2–1.5 m) cane should be inserted for each plant. Leave about 18 inches (45 cm) between plants to allow plenty of room for spread. The boxes of plants should be thoroughly watered the day before they are to be moved and each plant placed as near to the cane as possible. Do not plant too deep, just allow about 1 inch (2.5 cm) of soil to cover the root ball. Tie to the cane immediately to avoid wind damage.

FINAL POTTING FOR LATES

By mid or late May it will be found that most late-flowering plants have filled their 5-inch (13 cm) pot with root. This is easily checked by inverting the pot and giving the top a smart tap on the edge of the frame. If the root has gone to the bottom of the pot and is starting to go round the bottom then the plant is ready for a move. Use 8½- to 9-inch (20–22 cm) or 10-inch (25 cm) pots for the final potting depending on the type of chrysanthemum and the particular cultivar. As a general rule the incurved types are better in 8½-inch (20 cm) pots; singles in 9-inch (22 cm) and intermediate and reflex decoratives in a 9-inch (22 cm) or 10-inch (25 cm) pot according to the cultivar. Growers will soon get to know which size is correct by the root system made by a particular cultivar. Take special note of the root system when knocking a plant out of its pot at the end of the season; obviously those with most prolific root growth are the ones needing the largest size pots. It will often be apparent during the growing season which these are for they are the ones that dry out quickest and are often thirsty.

Here again the pots should be scrubbed and soaked before use. When potting leave 2 inches (5 cm) at the top of the pot for dressings of compost later on in the season. Again cover the root ball with about an inch (2.5 cm) of compost. Crock the pot well for good drainage is most important. Insert two canes and tie the plant in. A John Innes compost can be used for this potting but like many other growers of lates I prefer to use a mix of my own made up as follows:

> 4 buckets of loam; 1 bucket of peat; 1 bucket grit or coarse sand; 1 bucket bonfire ash and 1 bucket of old farmyard manure. To this I add 3½-inch (9 cm) pot of bone meal and a 3½-inch pot of chrysanthemum fertilizer.

The pots of 'lates' are then placed on their summer standing ground where they will stay until housed in September. They are usually placed on boards or tiles in rows between two strong posts. Their canes are then attached to two straining wires running between the posts. If this is not done it will be found by the time they have grown to 4 to 5 ft (1.2–1.5 m) tall in the autumn they are forever being blown over and rolling about the garden.

Shaping the plant

STOPPING

The term 'stopping a chrysanthemum' means the removal of the growing tip; this stops the continued upward growth of the plant. The plant's vigour is channelled into the side shoots and laterals or shoots then develop from each pair of leaf axils; these shoots will ultimately grow away into strong stems or 'breaks'. Each of these breaks will bear one bloom in the case of disbuds, or several in the case of sprays. Often eight, nine or ten of these will grow away after a plant has been stopped according to the number of pairs of leaves on the plant. The grower must decide how many blooms are required on a particular plant and then take off the remainder; four, five or six is suggested on plants for garden decoration or for cut blooms in the house. The size of the blooms will be determined by the number grown on each plant and it is entirely a matter of preference. When stopping a plant it is best to remove only the smallest of tips and the date when this is done is very important as this will affect the time of blooming. A good general stopping date is about 25 May in the south of England; or 10 May in the north of England. Sprays can be stopped on about 1 June and most of the late chrysanthemums will flower in November/December if stopped about this time. Keep a note in your gardening diary of the date each particular cultivar is stopped. Note the flowering date and adjust accordingly the following year for the date the flowers are required.

SUMMER TREATMENT

If there is a quiet time during the year for a chrysanthemum grower it must be during June – I know that in the second week in June every year I head off to find some Mediterranean sunshine. The plants are quite happy growing away as the laterals develop nice strong breaks. They need very little attention other than regular spraying and the occasional watering. Breaks may gradually be reduced to the required number and these should be safely and securely tied in so they are not broken by heavy rains or wind. As the breaks lengthen it will be noticed that small shoots develop in their leaf axils. These should be removed as soon as they can be handled with safety. The removal of these 'side

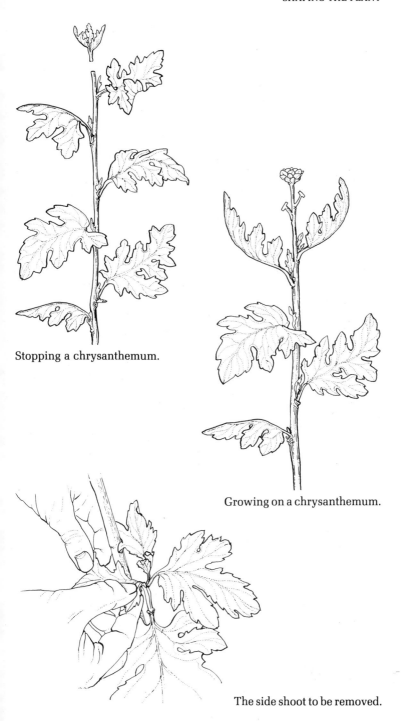

Stopping a chrysanthemum.

Growing on a chrysanthemum.

The side shoot to be removed.

21

shoots', as they are called, ensures that all growth is channelled into the breaks.

July is the month of bud formation and feeding. Every season differs, but usually as July progresses buds will appear on the top of each break and these in turn are surrounded by a cluster of other smaller buds. In the case of cultivars to be disbudded all other smaller buds are removed leaving only the main central one. This process is known as 'securing the bud'. The bud is now free to swell and subsequently develop into the bloom. As a good guide it is usually approximately four weeks from the time the bud is secured until colour is seen in the bud, and about a further four weeks until the bloom is fully developed. The procedure is somewhat different with the spray cultivars which are not disbudded. All side shoots can be allowed to develop and all the buds in the cluster around the central bud may be left to flower. In this way a beautiful head of flowers is obtained.

The feeding of 'earlies' usually starts at the beginning of July with plants getting a weekly feed of 1 pint (0.6 l) per plant of a balanced liquid feed. This weekly feed continues throughout bud development but MUST cease as soon as the skin over the bud splits to reveal any colour.

In the case of the 'lates' it is recommended that breaks be reduced to four or five per plant; for the reflex and intermediate types four or five per plant and for singles eight or ten per plant. Feeding of these starts when the pot has become full of root and this is usually about the second week in July. Unlike their early relatives, the 'lates' are given a dry feed in granular form. There are many proprietary blends of chrysanthemum fertilizer available and pots should be given a level teaspoonful once a week which should be well watered in. These pots will also benefit from a top dressing of compost placed in the pot. Two of these dressings, consisting of a good handful of sieved compost should be given, one at the end of July and the other four weeks later. Top dressing covers the top roots, encourages further root development and generally gives the plant a tonic. The buds of 'lates' are usually secured towards the end of August or beginning of September and at this time I advocate changing from the dry feed to a balanced liquid feed. As with early-flowering chrysanthemums, stop feeding as soon as the buds show colour.

Flowering and cutting

Colour appearing in the bud heralds the exciting time when flowers are developing. At this time particular attention should be paid to keeping the plants well supported; a flower head can be quite heavy and in addition to tying, some stems may need the help of an individual cane. Although the spraying programme should continue, ensure that no spray falls on a partly opened bloom as there is danger of marking the petals. Feeding is not recommended as the blooms open, as this could lead to rotting of the florets. Should the blooms be wanted for decoration in the house then they are best cut when about two-thirds developed and still with a lot of floret in the centre to unfurl. These will last for about three weeks with regular changes of water. However, should the more ambitious growers have his eyes on exhibiting a vase at the local show then the blooms should be left to develop longer on the plant. The longer the bloom is left the bigger and deeper it gets, although its life after cutting is not so long. Always try to cut blooms in the morning when the plants are fresh and turgid. Take a bucket of water to the plants, cut the blooms, crush a couple of inches of the stem and plunge straight into water. Do not cut the bloom and then wander around the garden bloom in hand for several moments before putting it into water; this considerably shortens the life of that bloom. After cutting, remove the bottom leaves and place in deep water for 24 hours in a cool garage or shed.

One of the greatest attributes of the chrysanthemum is the lasting quality of the blooms, and provided the water they are in is changed every few days they will keep fresh for several weeks. When the water is changed it is a good idea to cut the stems, thereby removing any calussing over that may have occurred. There is a variety of both dry and liquid products which can be added to the water to prolong the life of blooms but a good home-made solution is to add $\frac{1}{2}$ teaspoonful alum; $\frac{1}{2}$ teaspoonful Milton and 4 teaspoonful sugar, to $\frac{1}{2}$ gallon (2.3 l) water.

Housing of late flowering chrysanthemums

As previously stated, late flowering cultivars will remain outside on their standing ground throughout the summer and then be taken into a greenhouse to flower around the second or third week of September; this is generally when the first colour shows in the bud. From that time onwards the blooms need protection from the weather. The greenhouse should be prepared beforehand by giving it a good clean out and all the glass and woodwork washed down with a Jeyes Fluid solution. Then comes a most important task – before any plants are carried in, shading should be fixed up inside the greenhouse. This is essential, otherwise blooms will fade and scorch as the full heat of October sunshine hits them through clear glass.

There are many forms of shading, but without doubt the finest is obtained when muslin is fixed to the inside of the glass. This not only gives just the right amount of shading, but also absorbs any globules of moisture in the air or under the glass. Plants are then given a thorough soaking with a fungicide – in my opinion Benlate is the best – again taking care to drench both upper and lower surfaces of the leaves. Allow the plants to dry, then carry pots in to the greenhouse and arrange in the house as you desire.

It is at this stage that the enemy of the indoor chrysanthemum may attack. I refer to the 'damping off of blooms' which is due to *Botrytis* fungus. A close humid atmosphere should be avoided at all costs for this means certain trouble. The aim should be to keep a buoyant atmosphere at all times and an electric fan will help to keep the air circulating. Always keep the ventilators slightly open and in damp foggy weather a little heat will help to dry the atmosphere. If a temperature of 50°F (10°C) can be maintained in the house then troubles should be minimised.

It is important that pots are never allowed to dry out after they have been housed and while the blooms are developing. Watering techniques are now completely the opposite to those earlier in the season for now 'little and often waterings' are in order. Each plant will need about half a pint (0.25 l) of water per plant every day.

Spray chrysanthemums

The cultivation of both early and late spray chrysanthemums has become so popular over the last decade that I think it appropriate to deal with the cultivation of these types in further detail. The treatment given to the early sprays differs very little from disbudded cultivars in terms of general cultivation. First, it should be remembered that cuttings should not be taken too early – March is quite early enough. Cuttings taken any sooner tend to bud and flower much too early on short stems giving inferior blooms. Stop the plants on about 1 June, and allow four breaks to develop with no disbudding around the top of the branch as buds develop. Any feed should have the accent on nitrogen rather than be of a balanced nature, so as to keep the growth soft at all times.

With the late sprays there is no need to be in a hurry to get cuttings rooted. They need not be taken until June. This late date may surprise some readers but it is quite early enough. These June cuttings will flower in November and December at the same time as cuttings taken in March, but they will make a much shorter plant. Plants from March-struck cuttings will tend to grow very tall and become unmanageable.

About mid July when the cuttings are well rooted they can be potted on, one to a 7-inch (17 cm) pot or three to a 10-inch (25 cm) pot in John Innes No. 3 compost. The plants can then be stopped by removing only the smallest growing tip on or about 1 August. The three strongest breaks are allowed to grow from this top and flower on each plant. The plants stand outside just the same as the late disbuds and are housed at the normal time. As can be seen a 10-inch (25 cm) pot can produce nine colourful stems of spray which can be a great asset to any conservatory or greenhouse during the dismal days of November and December. Alternatively they may produce an abundance of cut flowers for home arrangements.

Charms and Cascades

These can both be used as a decorative plant when grown in pots and they will flower from mid-October through to December. The flowers on them are usually of the single type, the pollen carrying quite a strong scent. Plants of Charms often have a spread of three feet (90 cm) across carrying hundreds of flowers.

Seeds of both types are available from a number of firms and Suttons have specialised in these types for a number of years. If special types and colours are required they should be propagated from cuttings from selected plants for with seeds it is all a matter of luck. (Growing from seed is dealt with on p. 30).

Charms and Cascades make better plants when grown from cuttings. Rooted cuttings can be obtained from specialist chrysanthemum nurseries, but if any old roots have been retained cuttings should be taken from them in January or early February. As soon as they are rooted they can be potted into 3½-inch (8 cm) pots and subsequently on to 5-inch (13 cm) pots as stated for the disbudded types. When the 5-inch pot is full of root then the plant can be moved on into various size pots, ranging from 7- to 10-inches (18–25 cm) according to choice. Plants should be stopped when about 6 inch (15 cm) tall. From April onwards they can be put out into cold frames and then on to a standing ground. They are given a twice weekly feed of a high nitrogen fertilizer at half strength throughout the season. It is important to support the plants' growth by inserting about six 18-inch (45 cm) green split canes in a fan shape around the pot. All growths are allowed to develop and as plants burst into colour the pot is taken into a greenhouse or conservatory to flower. To get the desired symmetrical shape the pot should be given a half turn every day to ensure even development. The foliage on Charms is very susceptible to mildew and so regular spraying with a fungicide is recommended.

CASCADES

Cascades need rather more specialist treatment than Charms, and here again plants must always be given plenty of nitrogen feed to keep the growth soft. Plants naturally want to grow upwards towards the light and have to be trained to 'cascade'. When they are moved into the larger pots towards the end of May they should be planted at an angle to encourage them to grow over the side of the pot. They are then placed on shelves or in containers some 6 feet (1.8 m) from the ground. An 8-foot (2.4 m) cane is then run down from the pot at an angle of 45° to a straining wire 2½ feet (75 cm) from the ground. The plant is then trained down the cane. It is stopped at every second pair of leaves and the strongest break is then selected each time and tied in. About eight weeks before flowering time stop tying and allow the plant to grow on. Canes can be removed at housing time when pots are placed on a shelf or pedestal in a greenhouse so that the spectacle of cascading flowers can be seen to the best advantage.

Chrysanthemums being grown in pots
for the Christmas market.

Pests and diseases

PESTS

Prevention is better than cure! Never wait until a heavy infestation of any pest has occurred, for the plant may have become infected with a virus which has been passed on by any of the sucking insects.

Institute a regular spraying programme early in the season and continue right through to flowering as a preventative measure. However, should plants become affected with any pests, here are a few of the more common ones, their symptoms and control:–

Aphids (greenfly and blackfly). These important virus vectors are pale green, black, or reddish brown and are often first noted by their sticky honeydew excreta and the subsequent development of sooty mould. Spray with pirimicarb.

Leaf miner. White dots appear on leaves followed by twisted and curling white lines. Spray with an insecticide containing HCH or pirimiphos-methyl.

Tortrix moth. Leaves at the growing tips are webbed together almost like a small envelope. Unfurl the leaves gently, and remove the tiny caterpilllar from inside, or spray forcefully with permethrin.

Other caterpillars. Nibbled and damaged leaves or florets are the signs that a caterpillar is at work. Often the large black pellets of droppings are seen on the leaves or partly chewed florets found on the ground under the plant. Chemical control is not easy so hand picking is the main control although I have found that spraying with permethrin has deterred them.

Frog hoppers (or cuckoo spit insect). Found in a mass of froth on upper part of plant. Destroy by removing the insect which is in the froth and then spray with HCH or derris.

Earwigs. Chewed or holed florets in blooms are the trademark of earwigs. Here again permethrin can help, although mainly it is a case of hand picking from the blooms after dark with the aid of a torch. They can often be trapped in canes by filling the holes at the top with putty; or caught in an up-turned plant pot filled with straw and placed on the top of the canes amongst the plants.

DISEASES

Virus disease. Plants are stunted and leaves are invariably mottled. Pull up and destroy at once.

Crown gall & leafy gall. Irregular growths on the base of the stem signifies crown gall, whilst leafy gall produces clusters of malformed cuttings around the stem; there is no cure for either of these. Destroy the plants and do not propagate from them.

Verticillium wilt. A soil fungus disease. The bottom foliage withers and hangs limp to the stem. This spreads upwards through the plants. There is no cure. Destroy plants and dig out any infected soil where roots have been.

White rust. This is probably the worst threat to chrysanthemums and one that is relatively new to this country. It is most prevalent and the utmost vigilance should be observed with regard to this disease. There is a legal obligation to report any outbreak of White Rust to the Ministry of Agriculture, Fisheries & Food and it is most important that all growers should be aware of the symptoms. It is first seen as pale greenish yellow spots on the leaves; on the under-surface the spots are pinkish buff pustules. These often then get a whitish coating, from which the disease gets its name. The pustules contain spores and these spread the disease as the pustules burst. Anyone suspecting that their plants may have this disease should send samples of suspect leaves to the Ministry at Harpenden Laboratory, Hatching Green, Harpenden, Herts AL5 2BD for diagnosis.

Growing on chrysanthemums in the greenhouse border.

Chrysanthemums from seed

As mentioned earlier, ninety-nine percent of chrysanthemums grown are from rooted cuttings taken from stock plants. This way the grower is sure of getting blooms 'true to type' and preserving the colour, shape and type of the stock plant. This is not so with seed, but nevertheless there is a certain fascination about the uncertainty of the end product and many growers are irrestistibly drawn to try growing them from seed. The actual task of growing chrysanthemums culminating in the production of seed is largely carried out by professional growers, and although recently many amateurs have been entering this field, it must be appreciated that a lot of room is needed to grow plants and the proportion of worthwhile cultivars obtained from seed is very low indeed. However, there are now several nurserymen who sell seed, especially of the spray types and Charms.

As a general rule chrysanthemum seeds should be sown in early February in John Innes seed compost or a soilless compost. Cover the seed tray with a very thin covering of sieved compost and then water in with a fine rose on the can. Put the seed tray in a propagator at a temperature of about 50°F (10°C) and seeds should germinate in two to three weeks. They can then be brought out, pricked into boxes or pots and grown in the normal way. Charms and Cascades are often grown from seed and should be grown in their own particular way (see pp. 26–7).

Recommended cultivars

EARLY FLOWERING:

Incurved (Large)

Winnie Bramley (yellow)

(Medium)

Peter Rowe (yellow)

Reflexes (Large)

Pennine Snow (white)
Formcast (purple)
Solitaire (pink)

(Medium)

Regalia (purple)
Breitner (pink)
Yvonne Arnaud (cerise)

Intermediates (Large)

Ann Dickson (bronze)
Bessie Rowe (white)
Derek Bircumshaw (golden)

(Medium)

Murial Vipas (white)
Golden Julie Ann (golden)
Allouise (pink)
Angora (champagne)

Sprays:

Pennine Wine (ruby)
Anna Marie (white)
Lucida (yellow)

Margaret (pink)
Wendy (bronze)
Pennine Tango (bronze single)

LATE FLOWERING:

Incurved (Large)

Shirley Sunburst (yellow)

(Medium)

Fairweather (pink)

Reflexes (Large)

West Bromwich (white)

(Medium)

Beechview Flame (red bronze)

Intermediate (Large)

Gold Foil (golden)
Purple Glow (purple)

(Medium)

Alfreton Cream (cream)

Singles (Large)

Red Woolmans Glory (red)
Cleone (white)

(Medium)

Masons Bronze (bronze)
My Love (salmon)

Sprays

Romark (white)
Robeam (yellow)
Pink Gin (pink)

Tuneful (pink (single))
Milday (white anemone))

Charms:

Morning Star (yellow)
Golden Chalice (golden)

Bullfinch (red)
Ring Dove (pink)

The following cultivars are recommended for Christmas flowering in the greenhouse:

Shoesmith Salmon (salmon)
White Fred Shoesmith (white)
Mayford Perfection (salmon)

Sprays:

Elegance (white)
Golden Elegance (sport of 'Elegance')

USEFUL ADDRESSES

The National Chrysanthemum Society (Secretary – Mr H B Locke), 2 Lucas House, Craven Road, Rugby CV21 3JQ.

The following nurseries specialise in supplying chrysanthemum plants:

H. Woolman Ltd., Grange Road, Dorridge, Solihull, Birmingham B93 8QB.
Rileys, Alfreton Nurseries, Woolley Moor, Derbys. DE5 6FF.
H. Walker, Oakfield Nurseries, Huntington, Chester CH3 6EA.
N. Walker, Belvedere Nurseries, Chapel Road, Hesketh Bank, Nr Preston PR4 6RX.

Opposite: Above, 'Muriel Vipas', an early flowering intermediate chrysanthemum.
Below: chrysanthemums and dahlias growing together in a border.

Hardy perennial chrysanthemums

These chrysanthemums are the ones that are often seen in mixed herbaceous borders, and they are well worth growing for their abundance of flowers. Many of those listed below are available from good general nurseries or garden centres; the 'show' or 'florists' varieties which are grown chiefly for exhibition purposes need to be obtained from a specialist chrysanthemum grower. All the species, and their varieties, named below can be propagated by division, although feverfew is very easily grown from seed.

Chrysanthemum coccineum is known to many people by its common name of pyrethrum. The plants often need some support (i.e. peasticks or canes) in the garden, but they make good flowers for cutting. They prefer sunny conditions and a well-drained soil. There are many hybrid varieties available with both single and double flowers in wide range of colours.

C. maximum (the Shasta daisy), is a popular, fairly vigorous species which usually needs some support in the garden. It has large, single white daisy flowers with a golden centre, and there are several named varieties which have semi-double or double blooms.

C. parthenium (feverfew). This plant is a native of Britain; it is a rather short lived perennial and is in fact sometimes grown as an annual – it seeds itself freely. Small white flowers are borne during summer and autumn, and the aromatic leaves are reputed to alleviate migraine. Feverfew will thrive in any ordinary soil and prefers a sunny position. Several varieties are available, including one with double flowers and another with golden leaves.

C. uliginosum or **C. serotinum** (moon daisy). This species is tall (up to 6ft (1.8 m)) and bears sprays of large white daisy flowers in the autumn. It prefers a rather moist soil and will tolerate some shade.

Annual chrysanthemums

With the exception of C. *frutescens*, the following species and their varieties are all hardy and can be grown from seed for use as bedding plants or as pot plants. Generally speaking, a fertile, well-drained soil and a sunny position will produce the best results. Seed is usually sown in the autumn and the resultant seedlings are grown on in a cool greenhouse for planting out in the spring.

Chrysanthemum carinatum bears single flowers from summer to autumn; there are numerous named varieties available in several different colours.

C. coronarium grows up to 4 feet (1.2 m) tall and has single, semi-double, or double flowers which are borne during the summer. There are several named varieties available – those and the species are in shades of yellow and white.

C. frutescens is really a perennial species but as it originates from the Canary Islands it is not hardy in Britain and is therefore usually treated as an annual. It is often grown as an annual pot plant, or used in summer bedding schemes. The flowers, which are white or yellow, are borne from late spring to autumn. This species is grown from cuttings taken in February.

C. multicaule is a dwarf, compact plant, with glaucous leaves and single yellow flowers in July – August.

C. parthenium (see p. 34).

C. segetum (corn marigold). This species is a native of Britain and grows to a height of about 18 inches (45 cm). It has glaucous leaves and single yellow flowers which are borne from June to September. There are some named varieties available.

Hybrids between C. *carinatum* and C. *coronarium* are sometimes known as C. × *spectabile*. Single flowers of various colours are borne from June to September.

Opposite: 'La Cierva' belongs to the collerette group of dahlias.
Above: 'Kung-Fu', a small decorative type.

Dahlias

Introduction

The dahlia is one of the most useful and popular of our summer flowers. It would be hard to imagine a year without the appearance of this versatile subject, which offers a choice of characters to cover the requirements of the average gardener. If your need is for cut flowers, then the dahlia offers form and colour in wide diversity, from low-growing, compact types for edging your border to long-stemmed blooms of charming elegance that can grace your home. Colour runs dramatically from the whites and creams through a host of pastel shades to the deep, thunderlike purples, missing only the elusive blue which, it is fair to comment, is adequately covered by the wide selection of lilacs, mauves and lavender hues!

Bloom sizes are always a fascination to the new dahlia grower – the smallest blooms are only an inch (2.5 cm) in diameter with the largest growing readily to a foot (30 cm) or more in diameter, and with so much depth that the mature bloom resembles the size and form of a football. If such massive flowers are not for you, then the intriguing variance of form will offer single, open-centred blooms, those that have broad, flat petals – the *decoratives*; some with sharply pointed petalling, the *cactus* type, with yet another form, the *semi-cactus* varieties that have an intermediate formation. There are also globular forms that are known as *ball* dahlias which have tightly cupped petals, and in smaller sizes, the popular *pompon* types, sometimes referred to as 'drumstick' dahlias, so tightly compact and firm are the blooms.

As if all that were not enough, then you can choose dahlia plants with light green foliage, or leaves that are almost purple in colour and possessed of attractive forms from the broad spatulate to filigree pinnate.

As you will have gathered from all this, the dahlia is a hybrid, indeed it was already so endowed when discovered in Mexico by Spanish colonists in the seventeenth and eighteenth centuries. It is not without some regard for this ancestry that this flower is known officially as *D. variabilis*. The first seeds and tubers arrived in Europe towards the end of the eighteenth century, and the recipient, an ecclesiastic named Abbé Cavanilles, curator of the

'Evelyn Foster', a medium decorative dahlia.

Botanic Gardens in Madrid, experimented with the new arrivals in association with a young, Swedish botanist named Andreas Dahl who was studying with Cavanilles. It was the involvement of Andreas Dahl, and the work that he carried out with the Abbot in those early years that resulted in the flower being named after him. There were many exciting years to follow as the Mexican immigrant spread throughout Europe, and the leading growers of the time were quick to realise that here was a species to intrigue the flower lover of the day, mainly, of course, wealthy men and women who were always looking for something new in their gardens. So it was that the dahlia arrived here in Britain and became a firm favourite with amateur and professional alike. Today its fortunes are guided by our National Dahlia Society, the largest in the world, and, in conjunction with the Royal Horticultural Society, the combined N.D.S./R.H.S. Joint Dahlia Committee works to improve the dahlia by encouraging raisers and holding trials every summer at the R.H.S. Garden at Wisley (Surrey).

To appreciate the full range that the dahlia has to offer, the best idea is to visit Wisley or one of the other show and trial grounds situated in Britain, where you can see the plants growing and compare the many cultivars.

Above: 'Shirley Alliance', a small cactus dahlia.
Below: 'Athalie', a small semi-cactus dahlia.

Above: 'Davenport Pride', a medium semi-cactus.
Below: An example of a large semi-cactus.

Form, type and uses

As mentioned briefly in the previous chapter, the dahlia has a kaleidoscope of form and type that covers every requirement of the gardener in search of such essentials as border planting, blooms for cut flowers, or simply to create a summer garden full of attraction and colour.

To bring some order to this catalogue of beauty, most of the forms, their colours and sizes, have been classified by the National Dahlia Society. Here are the ten groups currently in use:

Single flowered: with a single row of florets around the open centre.

Anemone-flowered: blooms resembling the form of the anemone.

Collerette: single flowered, but each bloom bearing an inner collar, often of a contrasting colour.

Waterlily: fully double blooms, resembling the formation of the waterlily.

Decorative: fully double blooms, with broad, flat petals that occasionally twist along their length.

Single.   Anemone.

Collerette.

Decorative.

Ball:	globular formation, with blooms about the size of a tennis ball.
Pompon:	the miniature form of the ball types – blooms perfectly round on strong stems, some 2 inches (5 cm) in diameter.
Cactus:	fully double flowers, with petals that are long, narrow and rolled back.

Pompon.

Cactus.

A fine example of a ball dahlia.

'Polyand', a large flowered decorative dahlia.

Semi-cactus: blooms are intermediate between the decorative and cactus forms, with broad petalling in the centre to sharper rolled petals on the outer.

Miscellaneous: including any of the many unusual forms, such as orchid, peony-flowered, and those with fimbriated (split petals) form.

Within this spread of ten recognised forms, colour is classified into fourteen groups – including blended varieties (two or more colours intermingled), bi-colors, and variegated, where the colours are distinctly tipped, striped or splashed with another colour – a permutation here that covers every known hue except that missing pure blue.

Size varies from a mere inch (2.5 cm) in diameter to those massive giant-flowered types some twelve inches (30 cm) or more in diameter. On average, the size ranges between 4 and 6 inches (10–15 cm) predominate, but in the very popular decorative, cactus and semi-cactus forms, blooms named as mediums (6–8 in; 15–20 cm), large flowered (8–10 in; 20–25 cm) and the giants, which are categorised as any dahlia that exceeds 10 inches (25 cm) in diameter, occur.

Naturally, the smaller types, that is in plant height as well as in bloom width, are the best for bedding, and while a whole range of bedding varieties can be purchased as 'named' varieties, it is fair to say that the vast majority of dahlias grown to edge a border or use in bedding schemes are raised from seed, a method discussed in the next chapter. Several types of this low growing section of the dahlias repertoire are also suitable for use in pots or tubs on a patio or balcony. Best known of these are the Lilliput dahlias (sometimes known as Topmix or Baby). The compact, bushy plants grow only a foot (30 cm) or so high, needing no support, and cover themselves with a mass of tiny, single (open-centred) blooms just an inch (2.5 cm) or so across. Similarly, the **anenome** flowered varieties can be used in such displays, thus making this flower available even to those without a garden when pots are used on a patio.

The dahlias' value as a cut flower is legendary. There are few summer flowers that can equal the 'cut and come again' tag that this species has been given by those who have already discovered its versatility. Coming into bloom in July, even earlier in favoured areas of the country, dahlias will continue to bloom in vigorous splendour until the first hard frost of winter kills the tops. During this three months spell, a well-grown plant of a small or miniature-flowered variety can well offer the delighted gardener as many as 80 to 100 blooms; a very excellent return.

All types of modern dahlias have excellent stems — ideal for cutting – and with a little careful disbudding, a subject dealt with on p. 57, long, robust stems can be achieved with little or no loss in flower production. The best types for cut flowers are in the smaller ranges, of course, including the miniatures (maximum bloom widths of 4 inches, 10 cm) and the small-flowered groups, where mature blooms reach approximately 6 inches (15 cm) or so in diameter. The most popular forms for cut flowers are the cactus and semi-cactus forms, the decorative with their open, flat petal arrangement and the ball/pompon types. Contrary to popular belief, dahlias will last reasonably well in a vase after cutting, provided a few simple hints are followed.

Firstly, it is essential to cut dahlias at the right time of day; ideally, this is first thing in the morning, before the sun has reached them and while they are still full of sap. Second best is to cut late in the evening, when the blooms can be placed in deep water and allowed to stand in the cool overnight before they are arranged the next day. Always take a container of water to the plant, placing the cut bloom in the water immediately. When the arrangement has been made, place it carefully, avoiding such difficult positions as a table in a bright, sunny window or on top of a T.V. set.

In addition to the value of the dahlia as a cut flower, it can also be effectively used in the planning and creation of a summer border or island bed filled only with this genus. Imagine a curved plot that can be viewed from the window of your home and embraces the end of your garden. Tall growing dahlias, in bright reds and yellows offer a startling backcloth against which the medium varieties and then miniatures give a band of colour unequalled in its range. At the front of the display, seed-grown bedding varieties offer an edging that can be complemented by spot plantings of the elegant Lilliputs or Topmix with their inch-wide, starlike flowers. Perhaps you may think that such a planned border would be expensive and difficult to maintain. Not so – the dahlia is one of the easiest flowers to propagate, thus making it one of the most economical. And as for maintenance, the dahlia grows itself and requires no special skill to bring to perfection apart from the normal, pleasurable tasks that are associated with those who love growing flowers.

The massive 'Inca Dambuster', a giant semi-cactus up to 12 inches (30 cm) in diameter, one of the largest in cultivation.

Propagation

There are three methods of propagating dahlias – by sowing the seed; by taking cuttings from overwintered tubers, or by dividing those same roots into separate parts to make two or three plants grow where one grew before.

Most of the dahlias grown today are hybrids. This means that sowing seed to provide plants has its limitations. For example, if you wish to reproduce that superb red pompon that you admired so much last summer, then it would not be possible to do this by saving seed from the plant. Its seedlings would provide a great variation of colour and form, not the least of which would be a preponderance of single (open-centred) blooms, of little resemblance to the parent. To be sure of getting the red pompon you would need to take cuttings from or divide a tuber of the original plant, a method I refer to later in this chapter.

There are, of course, exceptions to this rule. The dahlia breeder in his or her search for new varieties will raise plants from seed saved from the previous season. Many hundreds (sometimes thousands) of such seedlings are grown in the hope of producing the results required, and when a worthwhile dahlia emerges from this horticultural host, it must then be from the tuber or root that the newcomer is increased.

FROM SEEDS

Seed sowing will be of value to the gardener who wants to grow bedding varieties. Dwarf bedding forms, with their single blooms and colour variation, are readily obtained in this way, and nowadays commercial seed firms offer different types of seed that will give a percentage of double dahlias (that is with a closed centre) and even some with dark bronze or coppery coloured foliage, a distinct advantage as it sets off in particular the bright yellow, scarlets and bronze blooms. If you wish to sow seeds, then they should be set in shallow trays of a good seed compost around the end of March through to mid-April if you are using a cool greenhouse, but a little later in a cold frame. Germination is fairly rapid – only seven to ten days are needed for the seedlings to break the soil surface. When these are of a size that is easy to handle, prick them out into deeper trays (or even individual pots) using John Innes No 1 compost or one of the useful peat-based

49

type, such as Levington or Arthur Bowers. In this well fertilized medium, the seedlings will grow rapidly, and if started in a greenhouse, should be moved to a cold frame, where they can become hardened off, before planting out in the open garden at the end of May or when all danger of frost is over.

FROM CUTTINGS

If you require a fair number of plants and would like to be selective about the colours and types that you grow, then propagation by taking cuttings is the answer. The procedures are very simple. Tubers of your chosen favourites will need to be set in trays (e.g. tomato trays) of moist peat in the greenhouse around the middle of February. Prepare the trays beforehand, and allow them a few days on the staging to warm up. Trim the overwintered tubers, removing any damaged roots and slicing away parts of the tuber that have rotted. Such cuts can be protected from becoming infected by dusting with flowers of sulphur. Push the tubers into the surface of the peat rather than bury them. The new growth will emerge mainly from the crown of the old root (that is the junction between the old stem and the fattened parts of the tuber), and it is this crown that should stand clear of the compost to avoid rotting. With a night temperature maintained at 50°F (10°C), the new shoots will show in 10 to 14 days. Water well when the new growth appears, and as the shoots elongate to around 3 inches (8 cm) in length, then they are ready to be removed from the parent root.

To induce roots to grow on a bare, severed stem needs several items and conditions i.e. seed trays or pots of a rooting compost (a good choice is 50/50 peat and coarse sand), a small propagator or enclosed area in the greenhouse to give rooting temperatures and bottom heat (i.e. heat rising from below) to maintain those essential temperatures. I prefer to use one of those dome-like plastic hoods that fit on a seed tray, which helps to maintain an even, humid atmosphere around the cuttings.

To achieve efficient results, take the cuttings very carefully from the old root by cutting with a sharp knife fractionally above the point where the growth emerges from the tuber. This means that you will leave the 'eye' to produce more cuttings later on from the buds left behind. Dip the cutting in a hormone rooting powder (obtainable from any garden centre or horticultural supplier) and insert it an inch (2.5 cm) deep in the rooting mixture. When you have prepared a full tray, cover it with the plastic dome and shade when the weather is bright and sunny to avoid wilting.

It takes around fourteen days for the cuttings to root, and they will stand up perkily when this miracle of nature has occurred showing that they are ready for the next step. This is a move from the peat and sand rooting mixture, which contains no nutrient, to something more acceptable to good development. As with the seedlings, use John Innes compost No. 1 or a peat-based compost for this potting on. Small, individual pots or deep trays should be used, spacing the newly-rooted cuttings 4 to 5 inches (10–12 cm) apart in the trays. Growth will be rapid from now on, and once more it is advisable to place the cuttings in a cold frame to harden them off as they start to grow. Keep a close watch on the young plants both in the greenhouse and later in the cold frame. Pests like the persistent aphid and voracious slug can be a nuisance – spray for the former and bait with slug pellets to deter the latter. Occasionally, plants in trays and pots will exhaust the food available to them. Signs of this are paling or a yellowing of the lower leaves, which condition can be quickly remedied by using a liquid feed when watering – for instance the popular Phostrogen or Chempak.

BY DIVISION

The third method of propagation is probably the most used of the three. Division of the overwintered roots is easy to do, it gives replicas of your favourite varieties and, best of all, offers two, three or four plants to cover your own needs and probably those of your friends too.

Ideally, the old tubers should be started into growth as for taking cuttings, but the process can begin much later – in April (using a greenhouse or cold frame) or on a sunny windowsill in

'Wootton Cupid', a new dark pink ball dahlia.

early May. When the growth points show on the crown of the tuber, it is time to divide it, and this can be done efficiently by cutting between the two most prominent buds using a sharp knife or small handsaw. With the root in two pieces, look for further chances to divide, always retaining some of the old tuber and crown and a little of the new root system. Each portion can now be boxed or potted into good compost or put out in the open garden, set on a bed of moist peat, 4 to 5 inches (10–12 cm) deep. The new growth will develop very quickly and when potted make fine plants for setting out after frosts have cleared. If set directly in the garden, then the growth should emerge late enough to avoid frost damage. You can, of course, replant the old tubers untouched, but this is not the best method of producing first class results as the multi-stemmed plant that usually results will produce blooms inferior to those grown by the other methods I have described.

Opposite: Sprouting tubers.
Above: Division of tubers.

Cultivation

The dahlia, it has to be said, will grow almost anywhere and still produce first class results. But in accepting this fact of nature gracefully, the diligent gardener will know that by good husbandry and seasonal attention, those results will be improved immensely.

If you are able to choose a particular spot where your dahlias are to grow (so many people are not – being bound by design or permanent features), then the ideal is a plot to themselves rather than in a herbaceous border where they have to compete for nutrient and root space. They love the sun, so choose an open site, and avoid planting near to, or in the shade of, high shrubs, bushes and trees; such positioning will only result in drawn or overlong growth and second rate blooms. The soil in which the dahlias are to be grown should also be assessed. Badly drained areas of your garden should be avoided, and if you have no other choice than a soil so affected, try and improve the drainage by raising the bed in some way. It is easy to raise the edge of a plot with a low wall or boarding, piling the soil forward as you dig to give at least a spade's depth higher than the normal garden level. In such an improved medium, the massive root system of the dahlias will flourish.

As with most garden plants the dahlia will benefit from being grown in a soil that has been autumn dug and into which well-rotted manure has been incorporated. If this is completed before winter sets in, then when the soil is worked again in the spring, you will find that not only has it been enriched, but it is easy to cultivate. At this time – about mid-April – it is advisable to add a long lasting fertilizer, and my recommendation is fine bone meal broadcast over the whole plot at a rate of 4 to 6 oz per sq. yd ($130–200 \, g/m^2$), forking this well into the top 2 inches (5 cm) of the soil, where it will be distributed in readiness for the arrival of the dahlias at the end of May. This reference to planting at the end of May is for green plants rather than tubers which can be planted earlier in the month. In truth, 'the end of May' is an approximation, and the real danger is the possibility of a late, damaging frost. In the south of the country these are usually unlikely by the last week of May, but planting should be delayed a little longer further north, with growers in Scotland waiting until the first or even second week of June before planting in the open.

If you are edging a border or filling a plot with seed-raised bedding types, then they should be spaced some 9 to 12 inches (22–30 cm) apart. They will need no support as they grow and flower, but by inserting a few twiggy sticks amongst them as you plant, they will hold themselves upright in windy conditions, and very quickly blend in with one another eventually to make a continuous ribbon of colour around the flower bed. Such colour continuity is easily maintained by regularly removing the dead and dying blooms to allow the following buds to benefit. The taller dahlias will need some support. Plants that reach a height of 3 or 4 feet (90–120 cm) can easily be blown over in strong summer gales, and at least one main stake or cane will hold the plant firmly in an upright position. This main support is best inserted at planting time. Varieties in the miniature and small-flowering ranges should be set at least 2 feet (60 cm) apart; the mediums at $2\frac{1}{2}$ feet (75 cm) from one another, with 3 feet (90 cm) between the large and giant flowering types.

If the canes are put in a few days before planting begins, it is an easy matter for the soil at the base of each support to be worked down finely before planting, and it is a good idea to fork in to each position a double handful of fine peat or (better still) one of the proprietary peat-based composts like Levington. This will give the young plants a superb start and, by helping the root system to spread quickly, offers earlier flowering – an obvious advantage. In all of this planting activity, one consideration must be uppermost in your mind – that of hygiene. From greenhouse or cold frame to open garden, watch at all times for some of the pests that will attempt to attack your stock. Aphids, both green and black, will congregate on your precious plants if you relax your attentions. Keep this particular nuisance at bay with regular spraying, using a good insecticide, preferably based on malathion. By regular, I mean once a week, and if you choose a certain day on which to do this, then you will have less chance of forgetting it: Saturday or Sunday becomes spray-day!

Nocturnal attacks will be mounted by slugs and snails, but these are easily contained if you use modern slug pellets. These are made from compressed bran (or something similar) into which a chemical, metaldehyde, is incorporated. For some reason, the molluscs find this combination irresistible, and having had their fill expire conveniently alongside the plant, requiring that you remove the corpses. A night raider that is more difficult to catch or control is the earwig. This pest, and its many offspring, the nymphs, can do an awful lot of damage. The regular spraying programme will deter them, but trapping and destroying them is best. You will need to place a few clay pots on the top of your

'Inca Regal', a crimson decorative.

canes or stakes. Each morning, examine these and you will find that the earwigs have sought refuge in the darkness after a night amongst your plants. So empty the pot's contents into a shallow dish of paraffin or neat insecticide.

Alongside your campaign to keep the plants free from pests, should be another that ensures your plants are never wanting for water or food. Water is essential: 95% of the dahlia plant is water, and it should never be allowed to want for this life-giving essential. From planting to first flowering make sure that the plants are well watered regularly if nature is not doing the job for you. Each plant will need at least 2 gallons (10 litres) of water when it is in full growth; give this every third day in dry periods, with half this amount for the bedding dahlias. Feeding your plants at regular intervals will also improve productivity, and you can do this by one of three methods. From June onwards, when the plants are growing fast, you can use one of the excellent liquid feeds, like Phostrogen or Chempak, which can be watered directly to the roots (a very speedy method this) or applied as a foliar spray where each plant is sprayed directly onto the leaf area which rapidly absorbs the nutrients. A third method is to apply a top-dressing of granular feed to the soil surface, where it will be taken down naturally or, if convenient, can be hoed into the top 2 inches (5 cm) of your plot.

To help each plant develop more effectively, they should be stopped early on, that is the growing point is removed, thus allowing the side shoots (breaks) to push onwards to form a bush. To help retain moisture in the soil a mulch of rotted manure, peat or straw should be laid round the plants in June.

By mid-July, or earlier with the bedding types, the first bud will be showing colour, even a few blooms making their welcome appearance. If you leave all of these buds to develop, then you will have lots of colour, but most of the flowers will be extremely short-stemmed, making cutting for arrangements very difficult. To overcome this problem, remove two of the buds that appear in the main cluster on each stem, and the result will be a much longer stem suitable for your vases. If you need longer stems for particular arrangements, then disbud a little further down each stem, which can give you stems almost 2 feet (60 cm) long.

You can now expect flowering for three months, provided the dead and dying blooms are removed quickly from the plants, and it will be the first hard frost of winter that ends the display, perhaps even into November. And, surely, there can be no better reward than this for the efforts you make?

Lifting and storing tubers

To lift or not to lift your dahlia tubers, that is the question. What is the value of digging up the dahlia roots from the soil? And having removed them, are they not in greater danger from rotting than if they remained where they were?

There are several answers to these questions, but dahlia tubers taken from the soil have a better chance of surviving the winter than those left in situ. In favoured parts of the country growers leave dahlia roots in the ground with some success, but they would admit to some losses, and even to devastating losses in a really bad winter. To say that tubers are in a greater danger when lifted than they would be if left in the soil is wrong, and only carelessness or complete neglect of the stored stock would result in a complete loss. Naturally, when you have taken your dahlia roots from the garden, they must still have care and attention if you wish to carry the majority through the winter; there are not many gardeners, and that includes dahlia experts, who would claim that they could overwinter a complete dahlia collection without any losses at all.

Lifting is most conveniently done after the first hard frost of winter. This may be quite late, and there may be bulbs waiting to be planted in the ground occupied by dahlias. So is there any danger to the tubers if they are lifted before the frosts arrive? The tubers start to fatten dramatically from the end of August onwards – by the middle of October they have reached the maximum size. Lifting before the middle of October therefore means that the root is smaller and probably immature; in such a state, it has less chance of surviving the winter than a root which has been given full term. There are other reasons for awaiting the frost, not the least of which is that blooms will still be plentiful especially if an 'Indian summer' is experienced in early October.

If you decide to lift the tubers early, then my advice is to box the roots very quickly, in a mixture of dry peat and fine sand, so that possible dehydration is reduced to a minimum. If you wait for the frost to end the season for you, then once the foliage has been blackened, it is advisable to start lifting the tubers, as a following heavy frost can do irreparable damage.

Take out the dahlia roots very carefully, using a spade. This tool is preferable to a fork, as the blade will slice any tuber cleanly, whereas a fork can make a jagged wound in the root if contact is made, thus allowing easy entrance of damaging fungus spores. To minimise damage, make several insertions with the spade around the stem, at a distance of a foot or so from the base. By the third or fourth insertion, the root should be easy to lift out, bringing with it a lot of soil but with little or no damage. Remove as much of the adhering soil as you can, taking great care not to cut or gouge the tuber 'fingers'. With the soil removed, the tuber can be taken under cover, say into the greenhouse, to dry out naturally on the staging. If the doors and window of your greenhouse are left open on good, sunny days, then after a week to ten days, it will be possible to remove the remainder of the soil from the roots, either by further gentle probing or by giving the whole a vigorous shake.

The roots now have to be prepared for winter storage, and it is care in this preparation that makes the difference between successful storage and one where a lot of losses are incurred. First, all surplus fine and thong-like roots should be cut away with secateurs or scissors, leaving just a compact clump. Next, reduce the old stem to an inch (2.5 cm) or so in length, and then, with a screwdriver or long 'keyhole' saw (an implement I use with great success!) bore a hole through the centre of the stem to emerge at the base of the tuber. Thus a clean drainage hole is created, and the root and stem will dry out thoroughly, minimising the possibility of rot from trapped moisture.

With the roots prepared, the final act before storing is to treat with a fungicide. Nowadays, many dahlia enthusiasts choose to soak the tubers in Benlate solution. I find that this is achieved most satisfactorily if a bucket of the mixture is prepared, into which the roots are immersed individually. After a few hours, to allow for the solution to dry on the tuber surface, they are ready for packing for the winter.

My choice of container for this is the tomato tray (with small legs at the corners) which is so widely used by gardeners. With an inch (2.5 cm) or so of dry peat in the bottom, pack the roots together, covering them with more peat. If you have trimmed them well, then six to eight tubers can be accommodated in each tray. Stack the trays as you pack away the tubers, which will allow air to circulate between them – an essential for good storage.

With the roots ready for their winter sojourn, choose with care the spot where they will stay. Basically, it should be both frost and damp-proof, because both are enemies of stored dahlia tubers. A cool greenhouse is ideal; or a garage with a modicum of heating. Perhaps your garden shed fits the requirements. Places to avoid include a heated conservatory, a spare room where central heating is left on or an airing cupboard. If you do leave dahlia roots in such unsuitable places, before the end of the year the

The South African 'Match', a small semi-cactus with white flowers tipped purple crimson.

plump tubers will have dehydrated to the point where they will be useless for propagation the next spring. During the winter storage period, it is essential to check the tubers at least once a fortnight. Signs of fungus attack will be indicated by the presence of a grey mould on the roots. This should be wiped away, and if they feel soft to the touch, then you can pare away infected portions with a sharp knife, cauterising the wounds that you make with liberal dusting of flowers of sulphur, or a further covering of Benlate.

If such attacks are persistent, it is probably the position of your store that is at fault. Choose another position, and by trial and error you will eventually find the ideal place for overwintering stocks.

By late February (if you are using the tubers for taking cuttings) the roots can be unpacked and examined with care. Remove any damaged tuber 'fingers' or evidence of rotting, again cutting back to clean tissue. They will then be ready to produce cuttings for you – or, of course, to be sub-divided later on to increase your stocks. Such is the vitality and generosity of the genus *Dahlia*.

Selection of cultivars

The choice of dahlia variety is so wide, that in any selection made there are bound to be numerous alternatives. If we accept that beauty is in the eye of the beholder, then my recommended list simply has to reflect my personal likes. However, there are other considerations that I have given to my selection, not the least of which are growth habit, floriferousness and tuber-forming ability. The majority of the dahlias on my list are generally available, but if there is any problem, I will gladly recommend a nurseryman able to supply a required variety if a s.a.e. is sent to me c/o The Royal Horticultural Society, Vincent Square, London, SW1P 2PE.

DAHLIA SEED FOR BEDDING DAHLIAS:

Coltness Gem: around a foot (30 cm) high, single (open-centred) blooms in profusion with a wide spectrum of colour.
Redskin: About 15–20 inches (37–50 cm) high. All colours, mostly single with some semi-doubles and attractive bronze foliage. This type has received awards from Euro-trade organisations.
Rigoletto: Only about a foot (30 cm) high, with some double and semi-double blooms. Early flowering.

NAMED BEDDING DAHLIAS:

This group of dahlias is ideal for bedding or using in tubs on a patio. Most are double and are best propagated from cuttings or tuber division (see pp. 50–52)
Lilliput (sometimes called Topmix or Baby dahlias) grow only a foot high (30 cm). Notable amongst these are: 'Bambino' (white/yellow), 'Inflammation' (bronze), 'Pinnochio' (blended red/bronze) and the well named 'Omo' (white).
Park Princess is a low-growing pink cactus. Popular with parks authorities because it is so easy to propagate and is very free flowering.
Rothesay Herald: Red tipped white for this elegant bedder from Scotland that has decorative form.
Butter Ball: Yellow, as the name suggests, another fully double bedder in the decorative form. Very prolific.
Michigan, despite its name, is from Holland. Low growing with a delightful blend of orange and red in the miniature sized blooms.

Above: 'Danum Pinky', a pink and orange medium semi-cactus.
Below: 'Dana Diana', a brilliant orange.

Border Prince is a very popular variety in lilac shades, as is its sister seedling **Border Princess**, which is a mix of yellow and orange hues.

Park Delight is white and makes a perfect foil for 'Park Princess'.

Piper's Pink. A British raised seedling, colour as name, has semi-cactus form and is another popular choice for bedding.

DAHLIAS FOR GARDEN DECORATION AND/OR CUT FLOWERS:

The best varieties for garden and cut flowers are those that bloom early, produce freely and have long, strong stems. Colour and variance of colour (blends, bi-colors, suffusions etc) are readily available and so is a wide choice of form and size. Perhaps the miniature and small-flowered range are the best of all, and within this section, where the dahlias have bloom widths between 3 and 6 inches (8–15 cm) you can choose decoratives, cactus forms, ball dahlias and, of course, the rarer types like collerettes, anemone flowered and the indispensable water-lily. Here is a selection that should contain dahlias to suit every taste:

Klankstad Kerkrade: A dahlia of quality and reliability. Needle-sharp cactus form in pale yellow.

Gerrie Hoek: A pink water lily – maybe the most famous dahlia of all time. Reliable for cut flowers.

Hamari Fiesta: One of the most colourful of the modern dahlia range. A decorative type, it is yellow tipped scarlet.

Catherine Ireland: A recent winner at the RHS/NDS Wisley trials. About the size of a tennis ball, a decorative in white flushed lavender. A miniature.

Melton: Another fairly new introduction; miniature in bright flame that produces masses of blooms from July to the frosts.

Doris Day is a bit of a veteran these days, but still gives a first class performance in almost any conditions. A scarlet, pure cactus.

Rokesley Mini is a compact little cactus, purest white and another with Wisley honours to its name.

Cheerio: I could not leave this personal favourite out of my list. A wine-red tipped silver on the semi-cactus form. Elegant, cuttable and, best of all, durable.

Match: A South African import but such a beauty. White tipped rich, velvety purple. It looks stunning in a vase.

Andrie's Orange. Another 'oldie' beloved of the professional grower, simply because it is so prolific. Colour as name, in the semi cactus group.

L'Ancresse is a new arrival and winner of a top seedling class at the National Dahlia Show in London. White and very well formed. A ball type, the mature flower is globular.

Wootton Cupid is another ball dahlia in dark pink with some white. It is equally at home as a cut flower or in the border. One of the best of the new range of modern dahlias.

Porcelain: A favourite of mine. This water-lily type has the delicate white to lilac hues of its namesake. A beauty by any standard.

Chimborazo: Of the collerette form, sparkling red with yellow on long, cuttable stems.

Mariposa: Another collerette in lavender-pink and white. A cool beauty that will delight the connoisseur.

Comet is in the very rare anenome-flowered group. A bright red, with tubular florets like a pin cushion in the centre. One with which to intrigue your friends.

Opal is yet another personal favourite. It is from Australia, a blend of soft pink and white with honeycomb-petal form. A very elegant dahlia indeed.

Giraffe is a strong mixture of bronze and yellow but the form is that of an orchid. Not a robust grower, but with the pink sport ('Pink Giraffe') to make a matching pair, they grace any vase or garden.

A FEW OF THE GIANT DAHLIAS THAT OFFER A CHALLENGE:

It is not everyone that wishes to grow a 'dinner plate' sized dahlia, but in case you are tempted to stagger your friends with your skills, then here are a few easy ones to start with.

Hamari Girl is a dark pink decorative giant that grows on a fairly low bush to widths of 10 inches (25 cm) or more. An easy one for the beginner.

Bonaventure is an orange newcomer from the U.S.A. (where many good giants come from). It is one of the biggest dahlias in cultivation and yet grows easily for anyone. Try it at the back of your border.

Daleko Jupiter. A mixture of red and yellow, this British raised beauty (despite the name) is a massive variety in semi-cactus form.

Super, a dazzling scarlet semi-cactus from Holland is a personal favourite. It grows very easily almost a foot (30 cm) in diameter.

Silver City is a white decorative that finishes up like a football. Another easy one for the new grower.

Reginald Keene. One of the most beautifully formed dahlias in cultivation. A mixture of orange and flame – such an eye-catcher.